You Have A Visitor

Observations on Pet Visitation and Therapy

you have a visitor

observations on

pet visitation and therapy

Renee Lamm Esordi

foreword by Alan M. Beck

Library of Congress Catalog Card Number: 99-90589

ISBN 0-9672532-0-9

Book and cover design by Renee L. Esordi

Blue Lamm Publishing
P.O. Box 87242
San Diego, CA 92138-7242

www.youhaveavisitor.com

Printed in the United States

to zoey, terra, moro, and michael

contents

foreword

Animals have always been used by human beings—first for food and then for transportation. When people began to live in villages, more than 15,000 years ago, additional roles included protection and companionship, and the animals began to share our homes. There is now considerable evidence that contact with animals has beneficial health implications for people. Early reports documented that animal owners enjoyed a greater chance of one-year survival after a heart attack, and more recent studies show that animal owners have improved morale in everyday living. In general, people interacting with animals experience a decrease in blood pressure and display overt behaviors indicating a more relaxed state.

Most people talk to their dogs, cats, and birds. The voice tones and style of speech used when communicating with pets resemble the baby talk used with infants. The facial expressions are, however, different. Those used with infants tend to be exaggerated, as if the parent or other adult was training the baby to express feeling with the face. Facial expressions used with animals are much more relaxed, more comfortable, and clearly indicate intimate dialogue. That intimacy makes touching, petting, and talking to a dog feel good: it relieves tension and makes you feel more comfortable and appear more comfortable, more relaxed, and more attractive to others.

This intimate dialogue is in many ways similar to the touch-talk intimacy people have with each other, especially children. When you comfort a crying child, you just hug and stroke and say very little, perhaps repeating a word or two, such as "there, there" or "all right" or "okay." When the pain is deep or the child is little, you ask no questions; you just comfort. With a very little child who is sick and restless, you may sing or hum, rocking his body against yours. Words are unnecessary; each is content with what the other is doing. Between people in love, there are times when comfort means simply holding each other and saying nothing. If one person talks, it is often without looking at the other, and the stroking goes on beyond the awareness of either.

It is not surprising that animals may have a therapeutic role for people. Patients who are unwilling to approach or talk to a therapist are able to reach out to an animal. After playing with, touching, and talking to the animal, they begin to talk to humans again. The presence of the animal makes talk safe, whether that talk is directed toward the animal or toward another person. In very diverse circumstances—with patients in a nursing home, with autistic children who have never spoken, and with disturbed children who do not talk at school—the presence of an animal has drawn speech from the mute. Not only is it safe to talk to animals, but for some it is exceedingly important because only through feeling intimate with an animal can they feel safe enough to reach out to another human being. At all ages, caring for an animal is a focus of nurturing and a source of comfort.

"A small pet animal is often an excellent companion for the sick…"
Florence Nightingale (1820-1910)

Long before there was any evidence that animal contact enhanced physical and mental health, animals were being used in therapeutic settings. From the very beginning, animal-assisted therapy (AAT) has paralleled the use of animals as pets and many of the therapeutic uses are extensions of the health benefits now recognized for those who own or interact with companion animals. Much of the early literature documents nothing more than fortuitous interactions with animals that happen to be present in a therapeutic setting. The animals were to provide a diversion or the joys traditionally associated with pet care. These expectations may be correct, as often the best "medicines" are appropriate concentrations of what is generally beneficial.

Historically, the first AAT programs were hospital settings for adults, but now programs are common for people of all ages. The first recorded use of animals in a therapeutic setting was in 1792, when William Tuke used farm animals in his York Retreat, an asylum run by the Society of Friends, a Quaker group. In 1867, pets were part of the treatment for epileptics at Bethel, in Bielfeld, West Germany. The first well-documented use of animals in the United States involved the rehabilitation of airmen at the Army Air Force Convalescent Center in Pawling, New York, from 1944 to 1945. Sponsored by the American Red Cross, the program used dogs, horses, and farm animals as a diversion from the intense therapeutic programs the airmen underwent. Few records were kept of these and other programs. Today, better records, and photography document the impact of animals in therapeutic settings. A constant in the photographs of animals in such settings is the sheer joy and even laughter seen in the humans involved. Laughter and feelings of joy are therapeutic events and are often facilitated by the touch and talking to animals and even their antics.

Those who care about people often also care about our companion animals. Now there are studies looking at behavior and physiological indicators of relaxation in the animals as they interact with people. It is known that most domestic animals actively try to be with people, presumably for the same reasons humans want to be with them—the comfort of the family, group, or pack. In good AAT programs, all benefit.

In sum, we should remember that it is well documented that people denied good human contact and interaction do not thrive. One way people can be protected from the ravages of loneliness is animal companionship. All indications are that companion animals play the role of a family member, often, a member with the most desired attributes. Ordinary interactions with animals can reduce blood pressure and alter survival after a heart attack. Pets, for some, afford increased opportunities to meet people, while for others, pets permit people to be alone without being lonely.

You Have A Visitor truly appreciates the wide range of AAT programs available. The text provides honest and balanced explanations of programs and the photographs capture their impact in ways that words cannot. The book documents a relationship between animals and people that benefits both.

Alan M. Beck

10

Not only is it safe to talk to
animals, but for some it is
exceedingly important because
only through feeling intimate with
an animal can they feel safe *enough to reach out to another human being. At all ages, caring for an animal is a focus of nurturing and a source of comfort. — Alan M. Beck*

As the animal is allowed to

greet the patient, the owner

loosens their grip on the

leash, always mindful of the

patient's comfort level, and

always responsive to the *communication so often facilitated by the presence of an animal...I wanted to capture those feelings of joy and relief that people experience when interacting with animals.*

preface

A few years ago I picked up a hospital brochure. There were photos of a dog walking the halls and sitting in patients' rooms providing support, comfort, and a familiar face. "What a great idea," I said to myself, having thought that pets were not allowed in hospitals. I inquired further on the subject of animal-assisted therapy (AAT), commonly referred to as "pet therapy," which can be defined as the use of animal visitation as an adjuvant therapy to—not a substitute for—conventional therapies and healthcare.

Animal-assisted therapy consists of pet visitation and pet therapy, although a distinction between the two exists. Visitation is an almost immediate pleasure accomplished in one or two sessions per month, while pet therapy is a long-term process, with designated goals, requiring greater repetition and commitment with at least one or two sessions per week. The concept of AAT in either form has existed as a structured business for years—organizations scheduling pet visits into various facilities.

But AAT doesn't always require a structured program. Many nursing homes have birds, fish, and other small animals that live on the grounds and give pleasure to their human cohabitants. Sometimes facility staff offer to bring in their own pets to visit patients or residents. Animal shelters often have volunteers take some of their homeless animals deemed safe on visits where appropriate. At times AAT takes the form of a simple request of a dying patient to see the family pet for the last time—as was the case, I was told, of a dying man who had asked that his cow be brought to his bedside window so that he could peer out to see it. At those times when security is relaxed and privacy is respected, a last connection can be made between human and pet.

AAT has only recently become more widespread. For as long as I can remember, signs saying "no dogs allowed" have often been placed prominently on facility doors. Now more and more doors are opening to the idea of AAT programs due to the efforts of administrators, therapists, volunteers, healthcare staff, and others who know what animals have to offer. It is this unyielding commitment that makes the uplifting and meaningful exchanges between animals and people possible for those who need it most, and that brings the education and awareness that institutions need to open their doors to the animals that comfort our lives at home.

There are hundreds of articles documenting the benefits of positive human-animal interaction. Many exhaustive studies prove the presence of pets can change our lives, emotionally and physically. I was intrigued at the amount of empirical evidence linking pets to greater patient well-being, improved healing, and lower incidents of death. During AAT visits, studies show a significant increase in confidence, self-esteem, motivation, and coordination, and a decrease in anxiety and blood pressure levels. Meanwhile, caretakers express relief at their patients' improvement, and staff members welcome a break from their routines.

During my research, I found great resources on AAT—how to volunteer with a pet, standards and practices, screening and certification, and its history. I also found that as with anything structured, the business of AAT has its policies and procedures. National nonprofit organizations provide information and the nearest locations for formal animal certification to qualify an animal for AAT. Dogs and their handlers can be tested locally by a qualified evaluator determining the volunteer team's (animal and handler) ability to tolerate various stimuli that occur in healthcare facilities. These organizations also provide guidance and education on starting AAT programs and dealing with issues of risk management, liability coverage, and relevant laws or restrictions.

On a more local level, there are volunteer organizations or clubs that gather people and their pets together to visit nearby hospitals, convalescent and nursing homes, schools, and many other facilities. Some cover a broader area than others and range from a few members to several hundred. Many of these local organizations independently screen and certify potential volunteers and their pets based on the national criteria. Furthermore, the volunteer team's first visit is monitored to determine the success of their participation in the local program. Not all clubs make stipulations that members' dogs be certified, but all maintain that the animals—dogs, cats, and other small animals—bear a record of good health complete with current vaccinations, and in general, be well-groomed and well-behaved. Often these clubs carry their own liability coverage for their volunteers and pets to preserve their safety and credibility.

When the opportunity came to photograph volunteer teams at facilities, I carefully watched the dynamics of each visit. Usually a nurse would inform the patient of a visitor. Volunteer and pet peer into a patient's room with anticipation and unknowing. Bewildered faces quickly change to pleasant surprise as the animal comes into view. As the animal is allowed to greet the patient, the owner loosens their grip on the leash, always mindful of the patient's comfort level, and always responsive to the communication so often facilitated by the presence of an animal. The exchange was almost always the same, and I enjoyed seeing it over and over—the curiosity, the wagging tails, the big smiles.

I began taking photos for this book in September of 1998. I'll never forget that first photo shoot. I was dropped off in front of a nursing home where the president of a local AAT club was waiting. Filled with anxiety, I had no idea of what to expect from pet visitation. That day was a blur. I was photographing people bound by wheelchairs and tubes. Hallways and rooms were filled with furry visitors—I couldn't decide which room to walk into first. It all seemed so chaotic, yet we moved efficiently from room to room. People with different backgrounds and experiences were joined together by a common love for animals and the unquestionable benefits they bring.

Throughout this project, I was faced with many different situations. I was invited to observe a psychiatric program during an AAT session, but not allowed to photograph for reasons of confidentiality. I was able to observe and experience what cannot always be captured on film.

I also had the opportunity to visit children's hospitals where children are singled out by trauma, illness, and other unfortunate situations that find them in continuous care accompanied by parents who have spent days without sleep, standing by their bedside hoping for a happier time. When the dogs entered the room, these children had huge smiles, parents were relieved and happy to see any positive reaction on their young faces.

Rehabilitation centers were also a unique experience. I observed patients who interrupted their physical therapy routines to reach out and pet the dogs which, I was told, encourages a range of motion. Petting the animal is such a natural response learned in childhood, if not inherent, maybe the will to reach out a hand overrides what couldn't be accomplished during regular physical therapy a day before. As some sat in their chairs depressed or lonely, alienated, or angry, a pet diverted their thoughts for a while.

I also had the pleasure of photographing a young girl beginning riding therapy which has been an exceptional addition to her standard physical therapy. Her ability to learn and focus increased immeasurably as she performed various activities on horseback.

Another particularly rewarding situation for me was observing special-needs children interacting with dogs and cats. As the children were placed on the floor, one at a time, their stiff bodies quickly loosened and their contused expressions turned into smiles as they mingled with the pets. Staff members helped support their bodies and guide their hands across the animals' fur.

For those faced with hardship, the pleasure of a pet's company can be at its most profound. For this reason, there exists volunteer organizations that deliver food and supplies, and provide veterinary and grooming services to the pets of people who lack the necessary resources either physically or financially. I accompanied a volunteer on one such home delivery, and it is clear that for some, pets provide the companionship needed to make each day a bit more bearable.

On another unique occasion, I had the opportunity to play the role of a volunteer for a day. I accompanied a group of volunteers, each of us with dogs, to visit a rehabilitation hospital. I felt like a veteran having watched so many times before. I took Murphy, a large Golden Retriever, for our visit. We approached patients in physical therapy sessions, strolling the halls, or taking a break in gathering rooms. I didn't know them, I didn't know what to say, I just let Murphy guide me. People reached out to him. They either reflected on their own experiences with pets or asked questions about the dog. I felt the joy it gave and wanted to walk up to everybody.

I learned that volunteering with a pet can be stressful emotionally. Many volunteers stagger their visits and often only choose facilities where they feel comfortable. At the same time animals experience their own stresses and may need a break from visits too. One of the biggest challenges in making this book was witnessing for days and weeks at a time the human struggle that ensues when health fails. There were moments when I had to leave the room, and my camera provided a welcomed shield between the subject and my emotions. Animals accept less-than-ideal human situations without fear and question. They see past the trauma.

My goal for this book was singular and clear. I wanted to record moments shared between animals and people in unique and powerful situations. I wanted to witness firsthand the change in a person that can occur within seconds when an animal enters the room. I wanted to capture those feelings of joy and relief that people experience when interacting with animals. I felt so grateful through the entire process as volunteer organizations trusted me to capture and communicate this personal endeavor. I hope that as a window into the process and experiences of AAT, this book contributes to an increased awareness about this important service.

Renee Lamm Esordi
October 1999

It all seemed so chaotic, yet we

moved efficiently from room

to room. People with *different backgrounds and experiences were*

joined together by a common love for animals

and the unquestionable benefits they bring.

acknowledgments

This book is a product of great teamwork. A project like this could not have been accomplished without the support and cooperation of many people who had faith in this endeavor.

Michigan

I am very grateful to Ruth Curry, president of Pet-A-Pet in Detroit. She had arranged such a diverse schedule during the two weeks I spent with her, not wanting to send me home empty-handed. Before each visit, she briefed me on what to expect, which established the groundwork for how I would process visits elsewhere with other groups. I am very grateful for her support and love throughout this project. I also thank her husband, Hub, for the meals between photo shoots.

I also thank Lori Clinton, whose dog Nell was used in a chapter to chronicle a day's visit. Lori's efforts, guidance, and friendship were invaluable. She reminded me that the journey is as important as the end product and helped make the journey easier in many ways.

Rebekah Shaefer's support during our conversations was very valuable, as well as her information and insights on her experiences with AAT and its benefits to her hospital program.

I am very grateful to all the volunteers at Pet-A-Pet for being available during visits and enthusiastic about the project.

Activities directors and staff were very kind to allow me access to the following facilities: St. Anne's Mead in Southfield; Camp Oakland Youth Programs in Oxford, Woodhaven in Livonia; Presbyterian Village of Redford, Old Village School in Northville, Oakwood Hospital in Dearborn; Garden City Hospital in Garden City; Cleveland School in Livonia; Children's Hospital of Michigan in Detroit; and Faith Haven in Jackson. I also thank Christine Clinton-Cali, Kelly Scheer, and Suzanne Chesney. I am also grateful to those who helped me with permissions and paperwork.

Mary Beth Gross was very helpful before and during my visit to her home. Our visit to a nearby nursing home was very memorable.

New Hampshire
I am very grateful to John Bryant, president of the Green Mountain Humane Society, for fitting in three wonderful visits during my brief stay in New Hampshire and also for his helpful advice and information. I also thank the GMHS volunteers that ventured out with their pets on a snowy day.

For help with permissions, paperwork, and references I thank Carolyn Sailer and Children's Hospital at Dartmouth in Lebanon; Ginni Balch and Hanover Terrace Healthcare in Hanover; and Dr. Michael Mayor.

California
I am very grateful to Robin Cohen and the Helen Woodward Animal Center, its volunteers, and staff. I also thank the Activities directors and staff of Scripps Torrey Pines Convalescent Hospital in La Jolla, and Beverly Manor in Escondido.

Lesley Nevers and Kristina Murden of Scripps Health were very helpful in their efforts to coordinate a visit at one of the Scripps Hospitals in San Diego county. I also thank Nancy Stern, her staff, Scripps Memorial Hospital Encinitas, and Barbara Richman.

Else Megeath, Steve Wayland, Pamela Magette, Nadia Sutton, and PAWS/LA were a tremendous help in coordinating a visit with one of their volunteers. I also thank Meredith Gibbs and Joe Monroe.

In general
When I started researching and making contacts, my first resource was Karen Buchinger. She researched and provided articles on this subject from medical journals and trade publications and pointed me to people who might be helpful in my mission. My sincere appreciation goes to Catharine M. Lamm for her editorial and written contributions, assistance with visits, and her support and advice in this project, and I am always thankful for her friendship. I am most grateful to my family for encouraging me to achieve my goals, for their support throughout all my projects, and for believing in me. I thank the Esordi family for their support, legal advice, and for their efforts. I thank Alan M. Beck for his time in contributing a wonderful foreword. I also thank William Clark, D.V.M., Retired; Michael and Diana Smith; Kathy Bankerd; Delta Society; Therapy Dogs Inc.; Therapy Dogs International, Inc.; Canine Companions for Independence; and the American Kennel Club.

To everyone who has given me support and advice throughout this project, both encouraging and critical, I give my thanks. One of the best aspects of this project has been the ability to discuss the process and share my experiences both good and bad to others. I am grateful to those who have shared their time and resources. I thank my husband, Michael, for his love and encouragement every day, and for supporting this project and making it a reality.

I am grateful to the people who appear in this book, for their trust and interest, and for allowing me to photograph them. I thank those who allowed me to do so. I also thank the owners of all the pets I have photographed. And lastly, I am especially thankful to the pets who appear in this book, and to all the animals for their unconditional love, patience, and support.

Who it was to first keep an animal as a pet

may be a mystery, but why they did it is clear in many ways. We are, after all, animals ourselves, sharing this planet with a dizzying array of other living things. So why not want to be close to some of them?

Still, human language does set us apart from other animals. We are in many ways more advanced, although we are not necessarily better off. Our speech is at the same time liberating and confining—liberating as an almost limitless tool for communication and invention, confining as words themselves can create conflict and hold us back.

The complexity of human language can also cause other modes of communication to fall to the side. Gestures, facial expressions, tone, and touch—other animals are experts at these. Touch especially can get left behind in the human experience. A hand on the arm, a rub on the back, fingers through the hair, a good long hug—most of us could use a little more of that sort of thing, and animals are one way to get it... and give it.

Pets, dogs especially, are tuned in to all those modes of communication that humans sometimes neglect. Compared to us, these animals keep things simple—a happy tone, a playful stance, a touch of the nose, and enough said. Pets have no room for those additional elements involved in human-to-human relationships including pity, scorn, judgement, and standards of beauty—all things we fear from our fellow humans. And it is when we are at our most vulnerable—old, sick, alone, in pain—that freedom from our fears can provide the most benefit. For some, animals give a rare sense of unconditional love. Exchanging affection with animals encourages people to be who they are and experience something wholly positive. And that makes people happy. And that makes people healthy.

Catharine Mayor Lamm

Molly and her owner, along with other volunteer teams, visit many residents
monthly at St. Anne's Mead, a nursing home in Southfield, Michigan.

Pet-A-Pet, Inc.

Detroit, Michigan

I read about Ruth Curry and her organization, Pet-A-Pet, Inc., in a Detroit newspaper. After reading the article, I wanted to meet her and learn more about her program, so I wrote her a letter. I didn't have to wait long for a response. She left a phone message saying she would be glad to introduce me to her program and its operations, share her knowledge, and take me on visits. We thought two weeks would be long enough to get a good batch of photos from various places. We had several exchanges by phone, and during that time she was coordinating visits with facilities and volunteer teams. Shortly before my arrival, I received a fax from a Detroit hospital. A friend of Ruth's who had implemented Pet-A-Pet into a therapy program eagerly announced her appreciation for Pet-A-Pet's contributions to the hospital program.

Anticipation and excitement grew for both of us. This would be my first opportunity to observe animal-assisted therapy (AAT). Ruth was anxious for me to meet her extended family of volunteers and their pets. I would be immersed in this very emotional experience, and have a lifelong friend when it was all over.

Running late on the first day of the shoot, I received a warm welcome from Ruth waiting for me in front of the nursing home. After a quick introduction, I was in a hallway filled with animals and people. It was hectic at first, until I walked into a room where a frail Italian woman was holding a kitten in her lap. I began photographing her with the kitten. She pointed out a newspaper clipping on a table by the window of her as a young operatic soprano who performed Sundays on a radio station. I could tell that performing was still a part of her. It was reflected in her movements.

I hadn't realized that hidden in these rooms are people who have had rich and full lives, and I was happy to have met her for those few minutes. Soon, I adjusted to the surroundings and began to fully witness the event of pet visitation. I was in and out of rooms, and was eventually led to a large room where residents gathered together. Dogs and cats filled the circle of people, and everyone had a chance to visit the animals. After an hour or so, we left the facility, and Ruth and I went to lunch. Finally, we had a chance to make each other's acquaintance and talk about her program.

As a result of Ruth's father being placed in a nursing home, she and a friend founded Pet-A-Pet, Inc. in 1986. Ruth had difficulty accepting the fact that her father lived in a home, and he and other residents would appreciate the idea of bringing kittens during her visits. "I wanted to do something. These people needed more." Ruth visited her father, and continued to visit, with animals in tow, for a year before he died. Her eyes filled with tears when she told me this story. Ruth also had the support of her son, a veterinarian, who initially told her about AAT and its benefits, inspiring her to start the program. A local agency temporarily provided the necessary liability insurance to take animals into facilities, and as Pet-A-Pet expanded, becoming more independent, the group was approved for a policy elsewhere. "We prayed it would be approved. We were scared to death." Her cofounder donated the money to begin the policy once the group was accepted.

Newspaper articles about the program and its services soon gained attention in the community. Not only were people asked to volunteer, but marketing was also used to promote the club's services and solicit those interested in starting an AAT program in their facilities. "We started to get volunteers. My friends would advise me to start programs here and there, news spread from the newspaper articles and by word of mouth, and facilities would call wanting us to come in with the pets. We also went around and talked to people to see if they wanted a program. I was really brazen."

In the last decade Pet-A-Pet has accumulated over 400 volunteers and visits more than 70 different facilities in the Detroit metropolitan area. Pet-A-Pet continues to grow into a large organization, yet Ruth is committed to keeping the club close-knit—a large family brought together by their love for animals, their need to help others, and a desire to improve themselves. Her goal is to not lose sight of the importance of volunteering. Although she cannot meet with everyone, she spends considerable time on the phone with current volunteers and those who are interested in joining, and she continues approaching potential facilities with her worn shopping bag of photo albums filled with examples of AAT.

Volunteering with pets offers the opportunity to share the experience with family members as well as giving the family pet a chance to mingle with other animals. This woman enjoys two visitors at once at St. Anne's Mead, a nursing home in Southfield, Michigan.

When volunteers and pets conclude visits with residents in their rooms, they join others in a recreation area (left) to assure that everyone visits with the pets. This woman (right) a former operatic soprano featured Sunday evenings on the radio, clutches this kitten brought in by a volunteer, one of several kittens waiting to be adopted from local veterinarians.

Court-appointed teenagers attend Camp Oakland Girls' and Boys' Ranch in Oxford, Michigan, for a second chance. These teenagers have faced difficult situations, and the camp helps them prepare for the outside world. The pets who visit offer these teens unconditional love—a chance to give and receive some much needed affection.

The teenagers at Camp Oakland Boys' and Girls' Ranch appreciate the pet visits. They enjoy walking the larger dogs on the grounds or sitting and talking with volunteers and their pets (left). This kitten (right) wasn't discouraged by the size of a Great Dane looming overhead.

Pet-A-Pet also attends special occasions such as a 2-year-old's birthday party where volunteers show children how to approach a dog, as well as entertain them with dog tricks. Dogs used in AAT are very tolerant in many situations.

This woman (left) holds the more affectionate half of this Boston Terrier duo, while the other half (right) rests throughout the visit here at Woodhaven of Livonia, a nursing home in Livonia, Michigan.

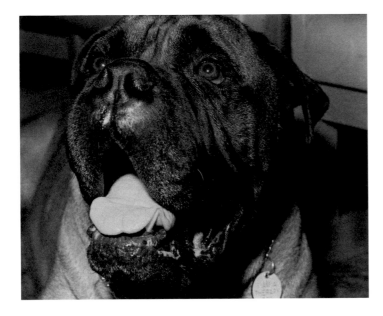

This Bullmastiff wants a little attention or a treat. Residents at Presbyterian Village of Redford, a nursing home in Redford, Michigan, enjoy the large dogs that visit. Several months after I had taken this photo I visited the facility again with Ruth Curry, president of Pet-A-Pet. This woman's health (right) had worsened since I saw her last, but her spirits lifted when I gave her this photo; she didn't stop looking at it the entire time I was there.

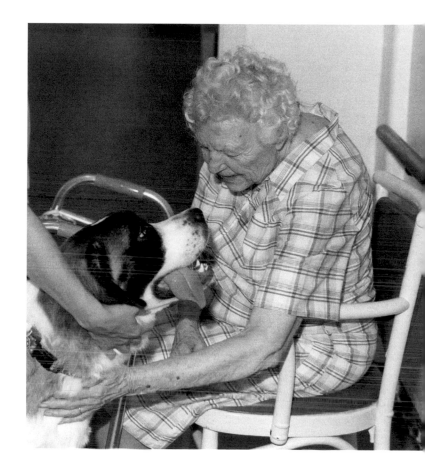

Visiting with the pets, residents at Presbyterian Village of Redford, a nursing home in Redford, Michigan, openly shared with the volunteers their stories of pets they had owned and the exciting journeys and interesting careers they had experienced in their youth.

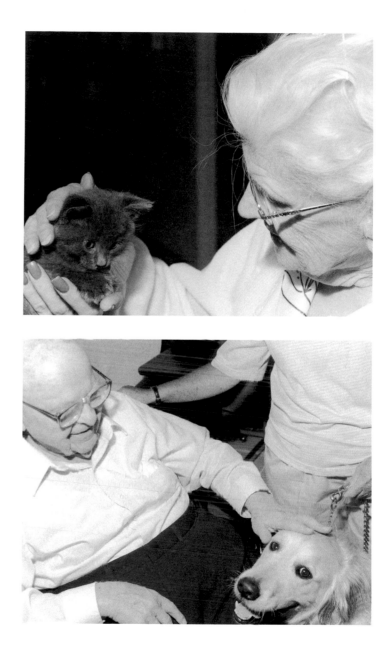

Dogs seem to communicate the same message to each resident, that of warm
reception and curiosity at Presbyterian Village of Redford, a nursing home
in Redford, Michigan.

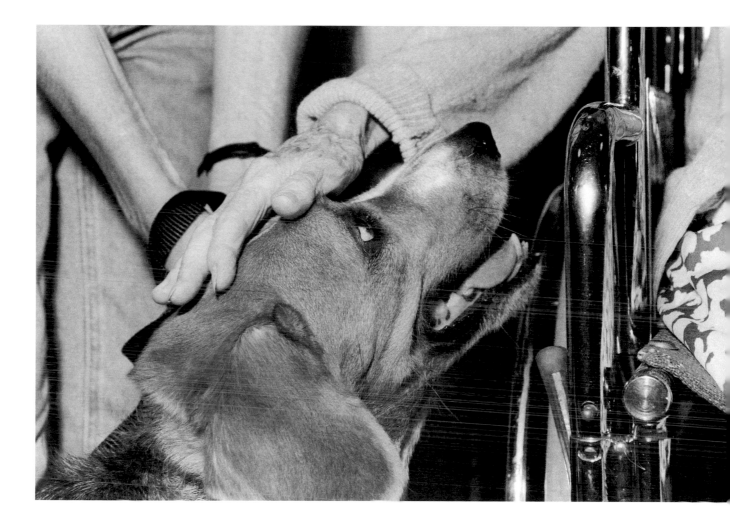

Improvements seen in stroke patients and others undergoing physical rehabilitation at Garden City Hospital in Garden City, Michigan, have resulted from the pet visits. Brushing Dylan (right) encourages patients to work on their coordination with the incentive of showing affection to a pet.

Working with Pet-A-Pet has opened up a whole new world of experiences and emotions for me...There was the woman who had suffered a stroke whose determination to grip Dylan's brush amazed me...There was the touching moment when a daughter rubbed her dying mother's hand with Dylan's paw...And I think most of all is the little boy in a wheelchair who waves his hands, swings his head, and squeals with excitement when he sees us, because he knows Dylan is going to pull him around much faster than he should.

— Tom Monolidis, Pet-A-Pet volunteer

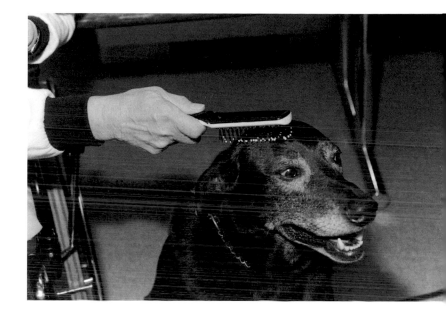

Pet-A-Pet visits a special education program

Old Village School, a public school in the Detroit suburb of Northville, was one of the first facilities to participate with Pet-A-Pet. The school provides education programs for special-needs children. Ruth was approached by a woman from the nursing home where her father had resided. The woman, having a special-needs child herself, asked Ruth if she ever thought of Pet-A-Pet participating in a special education program. The school's program supervisor, Christine Clinton-Cali, had been eager to start a program of this kind for years realizing the benefits the animals might bring to the children. Ruth quickly established a schedule, found a coordinator, and organized volunteer teams to begin visiting the school.

While visiting Old Village School, I asked Christine about her experiences working with the children and their response to the pet visits. Being a very cheerful and animated woman, her answer reflected an uplifting perspective: "These children are happy and will be children for the rest of their lives, taken care of daily, and they may never have to face some of the challenges that others dread."

She added, "Children with significant physical and cognitive impairments live in a very limited and sheltered world. Pet-A-Pet offers them an opportunity to experience a connection with another living being. I don't believe I truly appreciated the impact the program had on the children until I spent an hour with a child during the Pet-A-Pet visit. Watching faces light up as the animals enter the room, the children roll and creep to get closer to a favorite dog or cat and small hands grasp at the animals' fur, face, and ears. I realized how these animals bring joy and motivate the children to challenge their limitations."

A rescued chocolate Labrador Retriever is eager to visit and entertain special-needs children at Old Village School in Northville, Michigan.

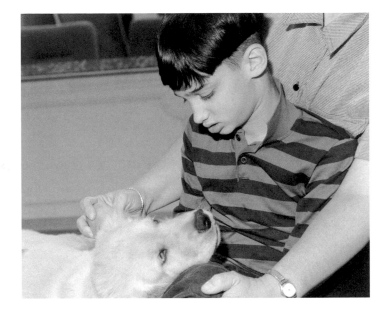

Norma, a Golden Retriever puppy and future assistance dog shows incredible patience and maturity at her age. Her "puppy raiser" introduces socialization at an early age to prepare her for future responsibilities.

Watching faces light up as the animals enter the

room, the children roll and creep to get closer to a

favorite dog or cat and small hands grasp at the

animals' fur, face, and ears. I realized how these

animals bring joy and motivate the children to

challenge their limitations.

— Christine Clinton-Cali, Old Village School

Among the several dogs that visit the school, Tyler, a 20-pound cat mingled with the children and the dogs like an experienced professional.

Pet-A-Pet visits a partial psychiatric program

Ruth was waiting for me in the lobby of Oakwood Hospital in Dearborn, Michigan while her volunteers and their pets were gathered in a waiting room on the fourth floor with Rebekah Schaefer, an Art Therapist in the psychiatric partial hospitalization program. Rebekah was joined by a few members of her staff to pet the dogs and cats as we waited for the outpatient participants to gather in another room. In the meantime, I interviewed Rebekah about the program and the benefits of the pet visits. Our discussion encouraged others to reflect.

In your opinion, do members of the group act differently when the volunteers visit?

Rebekah: Usually people have a positive response, triggering them to talk about their own past experiences with pets, and they continue to talk about it afterwards sometimes. You're probably going to observe that today. The pets often act as a buffer, getting people to interact more socially and verbally with others. Very rarely do I see a negative reaction. It's almost always something positive, and I think animals serve as an intermediary when somebody is afraid to verbalize to people. They'll be with the dog, and talk to the dog, and then they'll be talking to the owner and ultimately to their peers.

How often does the group meet?

Rebekah: They come in five days a week, Monday through Friday with six hours of program time. Many have been in inpatient psychiatric before they come to our program which may be a transition back into the work world. Sometimes they'll come from private psychiatrists who feel that they don't need inpatient hospitalization, but they think they will benefit from what we provide here. We assist our patients with coping skills. Most times when I present pet therapy I will integrate the group with stress management.

Rebekah Shaefer, Art Therapist, pets one of the dogs that visit the outpatient program at Oakwood Hospital in Dearborn, Michigan.

What are some of the functioning difficulties the patients have when they come to the outpatient program?

Rebekah: The majority of people that come in have mood disorders, anxiety, depression, thought disorders, delusions, and paranoia. Most of our participants are on medication in conjunction with the therapy that we offer in a group modality and one-to-one with their psychiatrists.

Staff member: We had a chronic patient that couldn't relate well to people, real negative attitude, not happy, assumed the worst in people, but with pet therapy, I saw a reaction in her that I had never seen before. She was open and loving and reaching out to the animals, and it was something I had never seen in her before. It was a real positive thing for her. She has two cats, but I didn't realize how much she benefitted from them being a part of her life.

Rebekah: People that have been rejected a lot in their lives or have a fear of rejection—it's so much easier for them to approach an animal where they know they're not going to be rejected, and they can have a communication with them that they're fearful of having with another human because they may feel inferior or think they have poor communication skills. It's easier to talk with others through the animal, they can connect with people even though they're doing it indirectly. It lets them practice some social skills on a level that maybe they cannot otherwise.

The one thing we always tell them, and we emphasize, is the responsibility that's involved in owning a pet. Because some people, due to their illness, can hardly take care of themselves, it's difficult for them to adequately care for pets. Animal-assisted therapy (AAT) gives them an opportunity to interact with pets here at the day treatment program and get a positive feel for it. We also discuss the benefits of owning a pet and the human-animal bond.

Staff member: And to add to that, sometimes their animal is their reason for being able to go on, to keep going, to keep reaching out because of their love for their animals—more than their love for people.

Rebekah: I treated a patient that was completely turned around in drug addiction because of her dog. She was addicted to heroin, and she had a dog that became pregnant. She was gone for days, when she came home, the puppies had died because of malnutrition. That experience turned her around. From that day forward, she never touched heroin again. It has been almost 25 years of abstinence. It was something that was so intense for her to see something sad. Sometimes people have to bottom-out before they have the motivation to change—well, that was her "bottom." Unfortunately the bottom can be something quite horrible.

I think the innate need to nurture is what is primarily therapeutic when our participants are interacting with a pet. So often here the patients are the recipient of care. It's nice for them to be able to give to the animal as much as the animal gives to them—to be able to give back a little bit is nice. When the pets arrive the patients can do some of the nurturing. You see a lot of behavior that you don't see in our patients otherwise. When I observe them with the pets, it's extremely beautiful to watch.

You see alot of behavior that

you don't see in our patients

otherwise. When I observe *them with the pets, it's extremely beautiful to*

watch. — Rebekah Shaefer, Art Therapist

How did you introduce an AAT program into the hospital?

Rebekah: It took so long...even with all the advocacy from Karen Battle, as our administrator. She was very involved in animal rights issues in the community and was an administrator at Oakwood Hospital/Merriman Center in Westland, a suburb of Detroit, at the time I was working there. It took a full year, she even gave me money to go out and furnish a pet therapy room. I think from the time we got it completely furnished, it still was another six to eight months before we were able to bring the dogs in with final approval from the Director of Behavioral Health Services. Jeff Cook, a therapist in the inpatient psychiatric program, had established Pet-A-Pet visits here [in Dearborn]. His opened shortly after the one at Merriman, since they're all connected, it was easier to get one started at the Partial Program when I transitioned here from the Merriman Inpatient Program. He works with patients who are hospitalized.

Jeff and I work together using the pets in our inpatient and outpatient programs. We initially introduced the policies and procedures that are implemented in the programs to the risk management committee at the hospital. Jeff was able to bring pet visitation to his program at Dearborn, with the cooperation of our pet visitation program at the Merriman location. It still took a while. I came [to Dearborn] in October and I don't think Pet-A-Pet started coming in until April—his took even longer than the one at Merriman because he didn't have Karen battling, for one thing.

What were the hospital's concerns?

Rebekah: It's biting, viruses, and infectious diseases they're more concerned about—dogs biting especially. At a previous meeting, we explained to them that often the bigger the dog, the more gentle. The larger breeds we have—Danes and Bullmastiffs—are our "gentle giants." There's always the liability issue. For some reason they still have that fear something will happen. We explained that Pet-A-Pet has their own liability insurance, but it's hard to get that through to them.

The pets often act as a
buffer, getting people to interact
more socially and verbally with others... *It's almost always something positive, and I think animals*
serve as an intermediary when somebody is afraid to
verbalize to people. — *Rebekah Shaefer, Art Therapist*

I left my camera in Rebekah's office and followed the volunteers and pets into the room where the outpatients were. They were quiet, reserved, nervous. While observing patients interacting with the pets, their voices became louder with anxious talk and laughter. There were about 15 patients in the room. The pets definitely brought out the patients' own animal stories, encouraging conversation among the group, from tame recollections to rather graphic anecdotes. A female patient in her early 60s spoke to me about the healing process on behalf of all participants. She sat beside a timid younger man holding a cat in his lap, stroking it with trembling hands, who shared with me that he has two Himalayan cats at home. The woman was talkative that day and very willing to answer my questions. I later learned that the two were not as extroverted the week before.

Do the animals help you reach out more—open up more?

Patient: Yes, because most of us here are depressed. In the early part of our sickness, we can't—we're inside of ourselves so deeply that we can't reach out in the beginning, as we get healthier we can reach out, but—see, the animal kind of forces us to come back up out of ourselves...we're far enough along in our healing. Like right now, if the dogs weren't here, I'd be sitting in this chair going like this—rocking. It made me come out of myself and love the dog...

Like right now, if the dogs weren't here,

I'd be sitting in this chair...rocking. — Outpatient participant

Our next stop was the tenth floor. The elevator stopped at almost every floor. Doctors and nurses shared the elevator looking at us and smiling at the dogs. Cats were carried in crates. A nurse got on the elevator and asked several questions about where we had been. She looked at Ruth and asked, "Can I get your card? I'd like to start a program on fifth floor oncology." Ruth had mentioned before we got on the elevator, "When we were in the lobby, a doctor approached and touched the dog. Seems they all gather around—something about animals that makes you want to stop."

We arrived on the tenth floor to visit with Jeff's inpatient group. Patients walked into a large room where volunteers and staff members waited for them to arrive. I sat and watched the patients interact with the dogs and cats. The atmosphere was more subdued, yet people tossed balls across the floor for the dogs to retrieve and held cats in their laps stroking them with a nervous energy. I focused on one man who didn't want to pet the animals or say anything. Instead he sat and watch the dogs play. He didn't take his eyes off them.

Nell has a busy schedule today.

A Day's Work

Nell visits two special places

Nell, a Golden Retriever of relatively small stature with a dark red coat, is quite a dog. Her eyes, like large dark buttons, never let you out of her sight, and are always aware and attentive to her owner, Lori Clinton. Nell's exuberance comes with an equal amount of patience, and her best attribute is her affection for others. Lori began volunteering at facilities with Nell in 1995, when Nell was just three months old.

Nell's energy could fuel an entire city for a week, but it is incredible how that energy can be completely contained when appropriate. I observed this transformation on many visits we took together. When Nell enters a hospital, she becomes very serious, mindful, and understanding of the importance of her duties.

Lori continuously works with Nell and has earned American and Canadian obedience and hunting titles. Her dedication to Nell's training is evident in the work they do together. Lori also has a 12-year-old Golden Retriever, Chelsea, who is retired from the show ring, but occasionally accompanies Lori and Nell on visits.

Nell and her owner, Lori, visit a classroom at Cleveland School in Livonia, Michigan, to demonstrate the responsibility and rewards of owning pets. The teacher there appreciates how much her students learn from these educational visits. (This teacher also enjoys taking her daughter and their dog to visit people in facilities.)

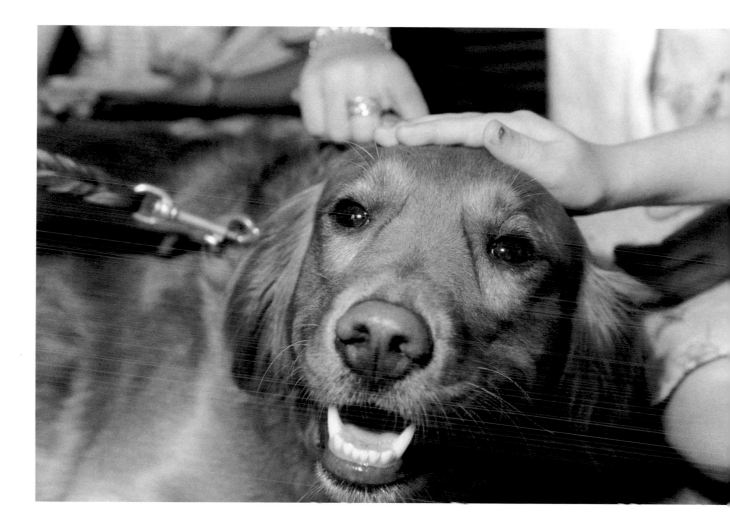

Nell visits a children's hospital

Animal-assisted therapy (AAT) at the Children's Hospital of Michigan in Detroit has been under the supervision of Suzanne Chesney, Certified Therapeutic Recreation Specialist, since 1988. A volunteer associated with the Auxiliary at the hospital approached her with the idea of bringing puppies from the Humane Society to visit the patients. Inspired, Suzanne initiated a three-month AAT pilot program on the medical unit. Prior to its implementation, she wrote a proposal and submitted it to the hospital administration and the department of infectious disease. "In the proposal I included a purpose statement, goals and objectives, a program plan, research to prove the benefits of AAT, and identified the minimal chance of complication and medical interference with the patients." The three-month trial was a success and the program was allowed to continue on a permanent basis.

In 1989, the program expanded to incorporate AAT-certified dogs, and currently uses only dogs that have been certified for therapy work by a national organization. In order to qualify for an evaluation at the hospital, the dogs must have passed the Canine Good Citizen (CGC) test. The CGC is a certification program created by the American Kennel Club (AKC) to evaluate a dog's training and demeanor in a casual atmosphere, to ensure that a dog has good manners at home and in public. "I then assess the dog," says Suzanne. "During the assessment, I observe how the dog interacts with others, and if the dog tolerates pulling and tugging. If a dog barks, growls, or does not recover from a startle, the dog is ineligible to participate in the program."

The dogs and their owners visit the patients room by room throughout the hospital. The dogs are allowed to get on a patient's bed, but they must remain on a leash at all times. Suzanne has two main goals for the program: "The first focus is to elicit an emotional response from a patient, to motivate a patient to socialize and interact, and sometimes to overcome missing his or her dog at home. The second focus is to encourage patients to reach, grasp, throw, walk, and communicate during individual treatment sessions with myself or another therapist."

While we waited in the lobby of Children's Hospital of Michigan, Nell
received attention from various hospital staff, and of course, many children.

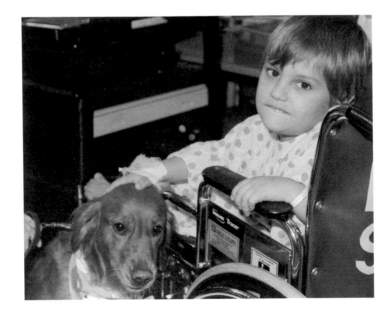

Children break from their activities, and video games get put aside when
Nell walks into the room.

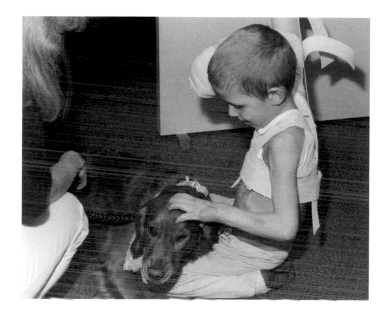

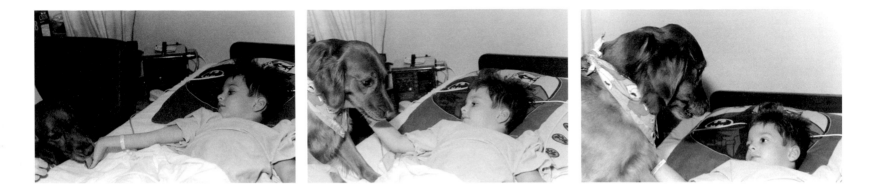

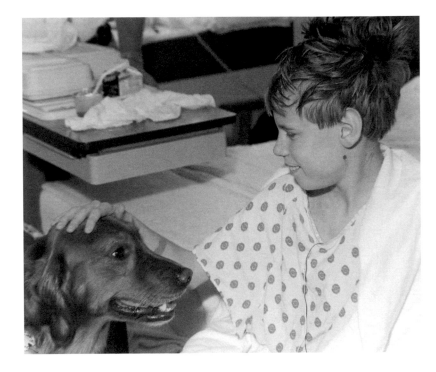

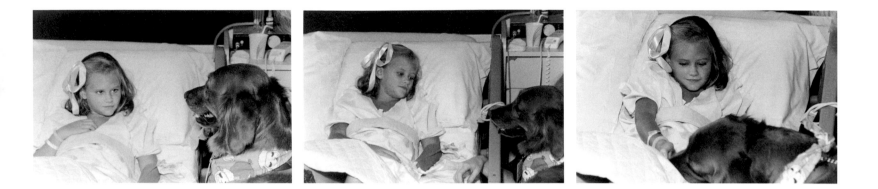

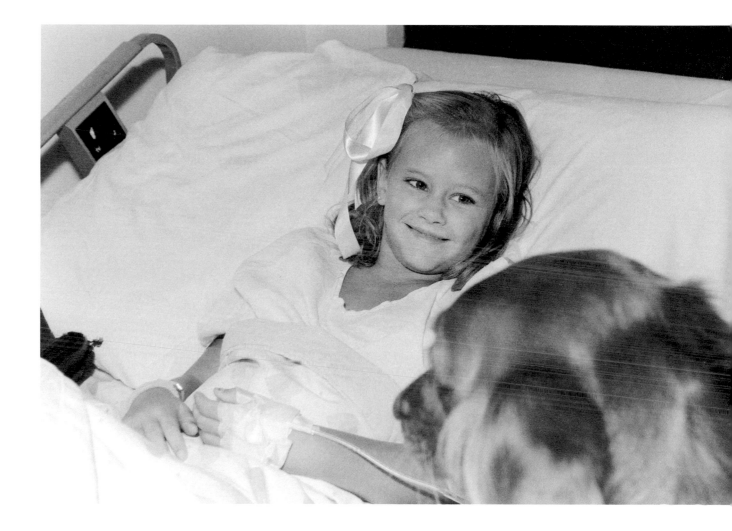

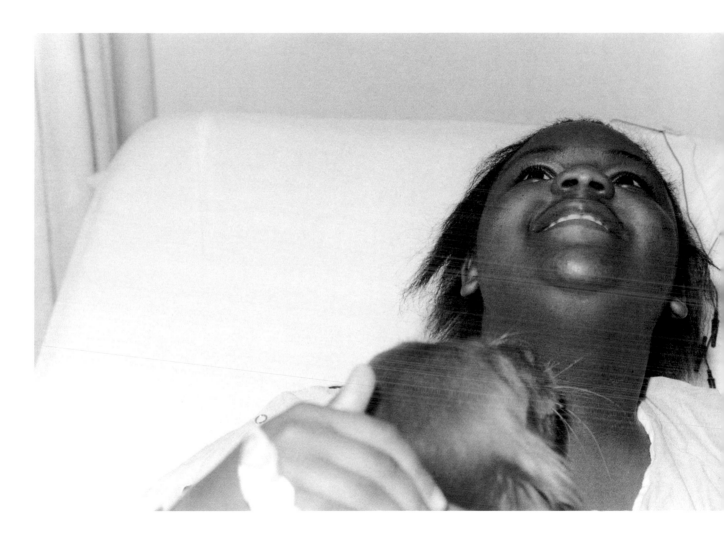

A dip in the pool is a refreshing way to end a day's work.

A sign-in sheet for volunteer teams is posted at Faith Haven, a nursing home in Jackson, Michigan.

A Sunday Drive

Jackson, Michigan

A friend told me about Mary Beth Gross, who has worked with dogs for over 30 years—showing, teaching, judging—is experienced in obedience training, and is also a nationally certified evaluator for potential animal-assisted therapy (AAT) dogs. I sent Mary Beth a letter about my project and mentioned that I wanted to meet her during my stay in Detroit. She responded with a brief history of her experience, the development of a pet visitation group she has started, and her observations and reactions to AAT and its value.

Her response was to my project, to say the least, inspiring: "Seeing a book on what can be done may put more dogs into the country's nursing homes and smiles on many more faces."

Mary Beth's involvement with AAT started with being a member of a dog ordinance committee and she became acquainted with the president of the local Humane Society discussing the need for AAT services in the area. She sent her Flat-coat Retriever, A-Me, to Flint to receive a nationally-accredited evaluation and AAT certification. When the CGC was introduced by the AKC, Mary Beth had been the local choice to evaluate dogs for this title, and after observing the extent of the evaluation—adding wheelchairs, crutches, and walkers in addition to the CGC test—Mary Beth decided that she could administer the test locally, and she applied to a national organization to be an approved AAT evaluator.

To evaluate a dog, she introduces wheelchairs and crutches, tugs at the ears and tails, touches feet and the rest of the body, and discourages biting and growling. If a dog fails the test, she works with the dog, encourages the owner to do the same, and when appropriate, retests the dog.

Mary Beth belongs to a small group of volunteer teams that visit local facilities. Reactions vary among residents in the nursing homes she visits; comments range from the negative ("Keep that thing away from me!") to the very positive. She remembers one man that would wait in the lobby for her and A-Me's visits. A-Me would retrieve a ball and place it in his lap repeatedly. The laughter was contagious.

She eventually retired A-Me from visiting due to the dog's arthritis, and her other Flat-coat, Chance, has taken over. She says he is nosy and needs to inspect the stuffed animals in each room. On one visit Chance was given a stuffed bear and paraded with it in his mouth throughout the rest of the visit.

"I think the dogs are a catalyst that encourages the residents to talk. With a dog under their hands to pet, I am told about the dogs in their lives and from there the talk can drift anywhere. Those who cannot talk, will bring forth brilliant smiles, as the dog's head creeps into their laps."

On that Sunday after we got acquainted, Mary Beth decided to take me on an impromptu visit at a nearby nursing home with Chance. The facility has a sign-in sheet and welcomes unscheduled AAT visits. We visited residents in the halls and in rooms one-on-one—not a part of a group of volunteer teams. This casual visit was unexpectedly emotional and had a considerable impact on me.

We casually walked down hallways and into people's rooms at Faith Haven, a nursing home in Jackson, Michigan.

I think the dogs are a catalyst that encourages the

residents to talk. With a dog under their hands to

pet, I am told about the dogs in their lives and

from there the talk can drift anywhere. Those who

cannot talk, will bring forth brilliant smiles, as the

dog's head creeps into their laps.

— Mary Beth Gross, AAI evaluator and volunteer

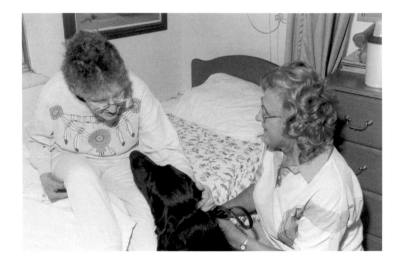

Mary Beth (kneeling) and her dog, Chance spent a few minutes in this woman's room. The woman was grateful for the company, and her kind words when we left reminded us that visiting with a pet is a special opportunity to help others.

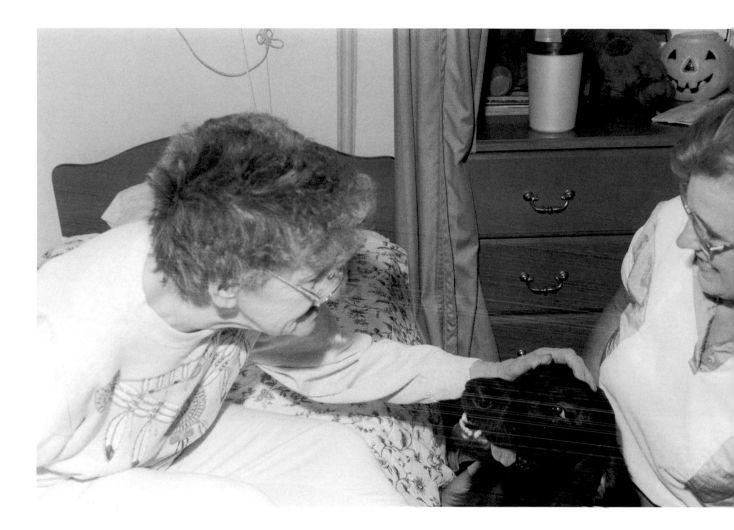

Farmer Brown (Brownie), a chocolate Labrador Retriever has many friends among the residents and staff at Hanover Terrace, a nursing home in Hanover, New Hampshire. They like to feed him treats when he visits.

Green Mountain Humane Society

Vermont and New Hampshire

During the last week of December 1998, I met John Bryant, president of the Green Mountain Humane Society (GMHS) of White River Junction, Vermont. We met on the campus of Dartmouth College in Hanover, New Hampshire, to discuss his organization, its services, and its unique involvement in programs and projects in both Vermont and New Hampshire.

As John began talking about his organization, his enthusiasm grew while recalling experiences in story-like cadence. He had prepared handouts for me with concise information, policies, and procedures. It was like being in school again. He explained and clarified much about the business of AAT. He emphasized, "To do it right, it takes a lot of time."

Staffed wholly by volunteers, GMHS is a non-sheltering organization providing a wide range of services and programs: pet visiting and therapy; spay/neuter financial assistance; enrichment programs for children that encourage the development of fundamental values; animal cruelty investigations; educational programs that promote animal well-being; and documentation including a formal declaration that assures continuing care for a pet in the event of the owner's disability or death. GMHS directs its programs to address problems in a way that minimizes the need for animal shelters.

GMHS has been providing pet visitation since 1989 and pet therapy since 1996. The program includes dogs, cats, and a llama serving senior centers, extended care facilities, hospitals, schools, and individual children with special needs. Currently, 45 pet visiting and therapy teams serve 21 sites and are scheduled to make about 700 visits during a year. GMHS prides itself on running a carefully crafted and tightly managed program to assure both quality and safety. All pet visiting and therapy volunteers are insured for liability by GMHS.

GMHS maintains a distinction between pet visiting and pet therapy and has different requirements for participating volunteer teams. Pet visiting typically involves a three-to-four hour commitment each month involving volunteers with hospital patients or senior care residents. The goal is to provide stimulating conversation, combat loneliness, and promote wellness. Pet therapy is a more structured program and involves animals and owners with children in special education programs. This program requires a commitment of about three hours per week while school is in session. The teacher and counseling staff are responsible for identifying specific goals they want to achieve through pet therapy.

Each pet visitation team is certified through a two-step formal screening and evaluation process. First, the owner is interviewed to determine interest in the program, and the animal is evaluated for temperament, behavior, physical appearance, grooming, and reaction to strangers, distractions, certain types of equipment, noise, and handling. The second phase of the evaluation is a coached and monitored pet visit to assess the ability of both the animal and owner to cope in a facility environment and effectively engage residents and patients.

In addition to the screening and evaluation process, pet therapy teams are also evaluated in a closely-monitored therapy session to assure that both the dog and the owner can function effectively in the special therapy environment.

Our visit to a nursing home in Hanover occurred just after Christmas and the snow was falling as we arrived. Walking through the front door, we were met by Farmer Brown, more commonly known as Brownie, a huge chocolate lab wearing a Santa hat. Brownie was full of holiday cheer waiting patiently to make his rounds. I readied my equipment and followed Brownie and his owner on their visits. He was an obvious favorite around the place. After sitting with one resident on the couch and sharing a few treats, Brownie concluded the visit by licking her ear, which made her laugh. Then everyone started laughing, and I could see John in the background with an approving grin. As Brownie got up to go, the woman on the couch said, "Thank you, that was fun...That made my day."

Brownie, a large chocolate Labrador Retriever, is a favorite with the residents at Hanover Terrace, a nursing home in Hanover, New Hampshire.

Brownie accompanies on piano as well as being a good friend here at Hanover Terrace. "Both pet visiting and pet therapy can evoke emotional experiences for both members of the team. The reaction of patients and residents can be moving," says John Bryant, president of GMHS.

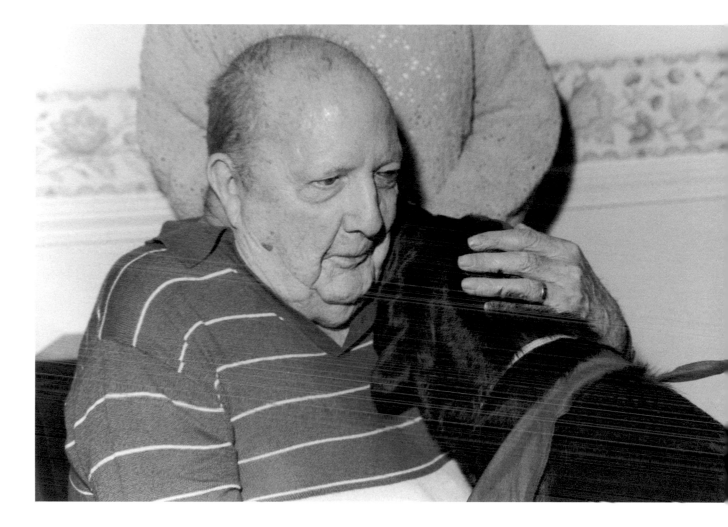

These cats enjoy being cuddled by the residents at Hanover Terrace, a
nursing home in Hanover, New Hampshire.

The Green Mountain Humane Society spreads holiday cheer

After contacting Carolyn Sailer, Child Life Specialist at the Children's Hospital at Dartmouth (CHaD), about her pet visitation program, I arranged to visit the hospital just after Christmas.

As I waited in the lobby amidst the holiday decorations, a Boxer named Seurat arrived in full Santa attire. The children were fascinated by this personable dog and her costume, and watching them pet her made me forget for a moment where I was.

Boomer, a Bull Terrier, later arrived for the second hour—a spunky dog who looked at the children with the same curiosity as they looked at him. Some of the children left their rooms to follow Boomer down the hall. They liked getting down to his level, which was pretty close to the ground. Watching Boomer's friendly antics with the children, his owner grinned and exclaimed, "I'm so glad I volunteer for this program!"

Said Carolyn about the program, "I wanted to incorporate pet visitation into our Child Life Program, which is designed to normalize hospitalization and promote psychological well-being among those in hospitals. Pets are a natural calming and soothing activity for many people, and it seemed like a great idea as one of our program elements. Unfortunately, I did have to jump through hoops to get the program established here, with many resistant to the program due to potential germs animals carry and issues of animals biting someone." She also added, "I do hesitate to get into the 'therapy' part of pets visiting the children and like to think of it more as a 'therapeutic activity,' such as art, and other activities the Child Life Program provides."

Boomer is a very funny dog, and he keeps children entertained during visits at Children's Hospital at Dartmouth in Lebanon, New Hampshire.

To get the program started, Carolyn consulted John Bryant at the Green Mountain Humane Society. In 1991, she wrote a proposal to the hospital's infectious disease and safety committee, which was rejected. After years of pitching the idea to the hospital, Carolyn was losing steam, and John had to encourage her to continue. Together Carolyn and John then brought formal certification and insurance procedures to the table, and the committee loved it. A structured process is something hospital staff can relate to.

At first, hospital security was not in favor of animals visiting patients, but they later became Carolyn's biggest ally. John says it takes a lot of time and education for people to understand. Physicians also gradually became more enthusiastic as they witnessed the dogs' positive influences on their patients.

Since 1996, the pet visitation program has employed only four dogs. Carolyn recommends rotating a small number of dogs because those children hospitalized longer can look forward to seeing the same dog again. Overall, she is pleased with the program's results. "For the children who are physically ill but developmentally appropriate, the dogs provide a sense of home and joy, but it is the developmentally challenged that I have been most impressed by when the dogs visit."

When the program was evaluated after six months at the hospital, the committee was a little disturbed. John says, "They were disappointed that we didn't bring a dog to the meeting!" Other than that, the program is a success.

This boy finds himself eye-level with Seurat, a very personable dog to the children at Children's Hospital at Dartmouth.

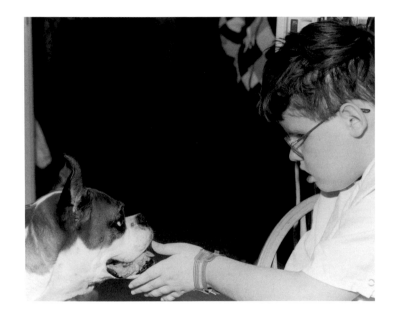

Child Life Specialist, Carolyn Sailer of Children's Hospital at Dartmouth, recommends rotating a small number of dogs because those children hospitalized longer can look forward to seeing the same dog again.

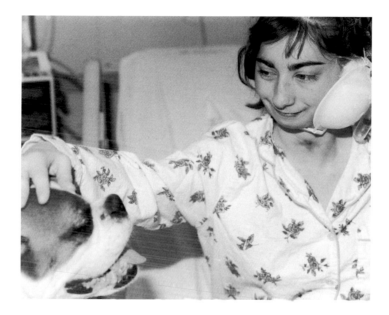

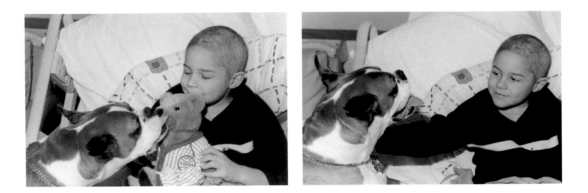

Watching Boomer's friendly antics with the children, his owner grinned and
exclaimed, "I'm so glad I volunteer for this program!"

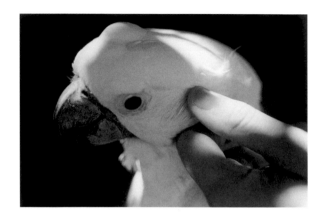

Harriet, an Umbrella Cockatoo, resides at Helen Woodward Animal Center along with other birds, rabbits, guinea pigs, and snakes. Volunteers from the Center take these small animals to facilities. Harriet is a favorite because of her responsiveness to human affection.

Helen Woodward Animal Center

San Diego, California

In 1972, Helen Woodward, a California native involved in charities for animals, the blind, and the elderly, envisioned a place where "people help animals and animals help people." This is now the mission of the Helen Woodward Animal Center, enriching the community with human and animal programs, and providing services that give joy and unconditional love to thousands while offering many opportunities for everyone to participate. The Center provides animal adoptions, Pet Encounter Therapy (PET—pet visitation and therapy), AniMeals (the delivery of pet food to the homebound), Club Pet (pet boarding), a community equine hospital, therapeutic horseback riding, education including programs for children, and group tours.

I accompanied Robin Cohen, public services manager in charge of PET, AniMeals, and riding therapy at the Center, on nursing home visits with several of her volunteer teams, and watched a client during a riding therapy session. Being at the Center is quite an experience. Daily stresses left behind, I was in a calming place where animals outnumber people. Everywhere I turned there were animals looking back at me, more varieties than I had imagined. I went to the Center on many occasions, as an excuse I think, just to be there.

In 1983, volunteers from the Center started visiting nursing homes about once a week with a couple of bunnies living in the adoptions building. "Back then it was a little more difficult to get acceptance into facilities. This was a relatively new service that could be provided to clients. Some hospitals were a little hesitant to have animals coming through. Nowadays we travel to 40 facilities a month with a waiting list of over 30 facilities begging for us to visit. So it's really grown as an accepted form of therapeutic interaction. We have over 60 volunteers in PET, about half of those volunteers use their own dogs or cats. Occasionally we've had birds come into the program. The rest of our volunteers use our small animals to take out on visits—rabbits, guinea pigs, snakes."

With a staff of 75, the Center also relies heavily on its 550 volunteers to support its services, programs, and special events, and to help with the care and grooming of its many animal residents. "The volunteers come in and they walk the dogs, they work with the horses, they give love and life to this facility," says Robin.

I asked her what she looks for in a volunteer team and how she works with both the animals and their owners or handlers: "First, the volunteers go through quite extensive training to ensure that they're a good match for the program. There is an orientation which gives an overview of the whole Center. They interview with our volunteer coordinator, and I'll introduce them to the animals and staff. I give them a copy of our visiting protocol—before the visit, after the visit, descriptions of disabilities and populations that we work with, and a couple of poems that convey our mission.

The first time volunteers go out, they're with me—shadowing me, watching how I conduct the visit. It's intimidating to go into these facilities so I always want to make sure they're comfortable. It's important that they observe how I approach and interact with the client—good eye contact with the client is important. Then, if the volunteers feel comfortable, they can take one of our animals on the visit. If they don't, I'll pair them with an experienced volunteer so they can see different techniques. It may take them three or four visits before they ever hold an animal and show it to a client. Everyone's different and everyone has a different comfort level; it's not for everyone. It's emotional work, and we have lost some people after one visit because they just don't feel comfortable doing this. I can't imagine doing anything else. If you love people and animals, it's the perfect marriage of the two—very special.

"As for dogs and cats, they have to pass a physical exam and have their program qualifications documented. Dogs go through a certification process where we test their comfort levels with different environments. I lift up their tail, look at their lips, pick up their paw, goose them from behind—anything that could happen in a facility. I test their tolerance for noise such as a dropped bedpan or an intravenous pole that rattles by. We take them around someone sitting in a wheelchair acting unusual, or we'll have a person cry out. We're not looking for a dog who doesn't react, just a dog who is comfortable and has a short recovery time so they can say, 'You've just dropped your plate of food, that's okay with me.' They must be comfortable around other animals and be able to resist food or medication dropped on the floor. They must also listen to their owners and follow commands well. I want the dog to enjoy these visits. If not, or if I see the dog is hesitant, I'll tell the owner that this dog needs more self confidence, do some agility courses and work the dog into enjoying it. While cats do not have to follow the same certification criteria, they do have to be comfortable around these same stimuli. We try to deliver the safest, happiest interactions that we can."

Besides dogs and cats, I asked Robin how the Center qualifies their other animals for the program: "Our small animals usually come from abandonment or neglect cases, or someone who can no longer take care of them. These animals are quarantined for 30 days to ensure that they're healthy and free of contagious parasites. They are screened by our veterinarian, and spayed or neutered to encourage a peaceful temperament. For a 90-day period, the staff then exposes the animals to the education classes, different people touching them, and different noises around the Center. Once the animals are ready for a facility, a staff person will take them out at least the first ten times to ensure that they're safe before going out with a volunteer.

"There's a constant dialogue between the volunteers and the staff. 'How did this animal react today? Were they uncomfortable with this population?' I want the small animals to enjoy this activity. We keep the visits to no longer than one hour. If our animals show stress, they get an automatic vacation of a week or two to recover. Interestingly, some animals get depressed if they don't go out. If our Umbrella Cockatoo, Harriet, doesn't go out at least five times a week, she will throw tantrums and destroy her house. She needs affection from the clients as much as the clients need her. Harriet

goes out often because she loves it, but the bunnies can only go every other day. If I have five animals going into a facility with 220 beds, I make sure that everyone who wants a visit gets one.

"Some of our animals will only go to certain types of people. We have some bunnies who only like seniors or children, some birds who only like adults. Harriet works with people who are paralyzed from the neck down. She'll cuddle against their cheek, which might be the only place that they still have feeling. And it goes both ways. We use so many different animals because not everyone is going to bond with a dog or a cat. A team member may say, 'he didn't like a cat, but he raised birds when he was young,' so we find the right animal for every single person. We get to know our clients and what they like, and volunteer teams are matched with facilities so that the animal enjoys and the client enjoys, and that's what were always aiming for."

Robin then spoke about the emotional side of being an AAT volunteer: "It's such emotional work. If you become too deeply bonded, you won't be able to last going out every week or every month see these people. Part of you remains safe inside while allowing a comfortable amount of friendship and compassion to come out. If someone has a very emotional visit— and there will always be those—they can return to the van with the other volunteers who understand what it's like. There we discuss things, we laugh, cry, talk about great things that happened on that visit, things that were difficult, and exchange advice. It's a great way to decompress."

I asked Robin about therapeutic riding at the Center. "We can help clients on so many different levels. An amazing aspect of riding is that it challenges those muscles used in walking. Traditional physical therapy doesn't offer the same benefits. We often use a bareback pad that has stirrups and a handle for balance. The warmth of the horse coming through the pad helps relax and loosen muscles and ligaments. And placing someone on a thousand-pound animal gives them a renewed feeling of control where they may otherwise depend on others to assist with almost everything. Riding becomes an empowering experience.

"Also, people have a different perspective from a wheelchair, or hunched over a cane or a walker. Being on horseback changes their perspective. Instead of looking up to people, people look up to them. This means a lot, and they regain a freedom of movement that we often take for granted. On horseback, we ask them to lean forward, lean back, reach out to put a hoop over a pole—exercising their muscles and their balance, as well as their mind. Or for a stroke patient who's forgotten certain words or letters, has trouble with sounds, or is unable to say colors, we have them ride across the arena to the letter or color block. They have to steer the horse, weaving in and out of poles and avoiding obstacles, which increases their coordination. When they successfully perform an activity, their spirit is lifted."

"Many of our clients, especially children, cannot compete in sports or play with others in the way that they'd like because of a slower response or motor difficulty. This way they're proud to be able to do something that most of their friends don't get a chance to do— horseback riding every week. We have a young girl in the program who benefits from the riding, she loves to do it, and is a really good rider. Her mother was in tears watching her ride saying that this was the first time she had ever seen her daughter excel at something and derive such joy from it.

"As for the animals, we use older, mature horses in the program. We need them to be calm, patient, and tolerant, and to know what signals to ignore, such as when somebody who has spastic movements kicks the horse repeatedly or tugs randomly at the reins. Like the small animals, the horses sense that this is special— that these people have special needs and the animals can meet those needs. They are exposed to all kinds of people, and they get time off just like the other animals.

"We also give something very special back to these horses. A lot of them have been injured, or they're high-performance horses past their prime, or their owners just no longer have use for them. These horses often come from a harder life than what they have here. We give them a second career—a chance to be needed without the pressure. People need to be needed, and animals are the same."

This American Fuzzy Lop rabbit is handled by a Helen Woodward Animal Center volunteer at Scripps Torrey Pines Convalescent Hospital in La Jolla, California. Patients and residents enjoy the variety of animals that visit monthly. This facility also has resident animals.

It's emotional work, and we have lost some people after one visit because they just don't feel comfortable doing this. I can't imagine doing anything else. If you love people and animals, it's the perfect marriage of the two— very special...If someone has a very emotional visit—and there will always be those—they can return to the van with the other volunteers who understand what it's like. There we discuss things, we laugh, cry, talk about great things that happened on that visit, things that were difficult, and exchange advice. It's a great way to decompress.

— Robin Cohen, Helen Woodward Animal Center

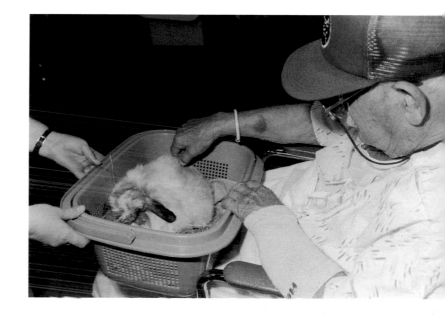

At Beverly Manor, a nursing home in Escondido, California, volunteers and
their pets visit people in the halls, a recreation area during break, or in
individual rooms. This hairless cat (left) is an interesting looking visitor,
while this dog (right) sits in this man's lap calling everyone's attention.

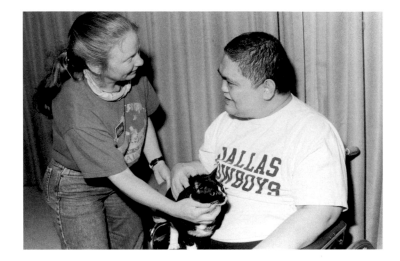

This volunteer and her cat, Isabella, visit residents at Beverly Manor, a nursing home in Escondido, California. This woman (right) loves Isabella to cuddle with her on the bed. She showed us photographs of her family during our visit in her room.

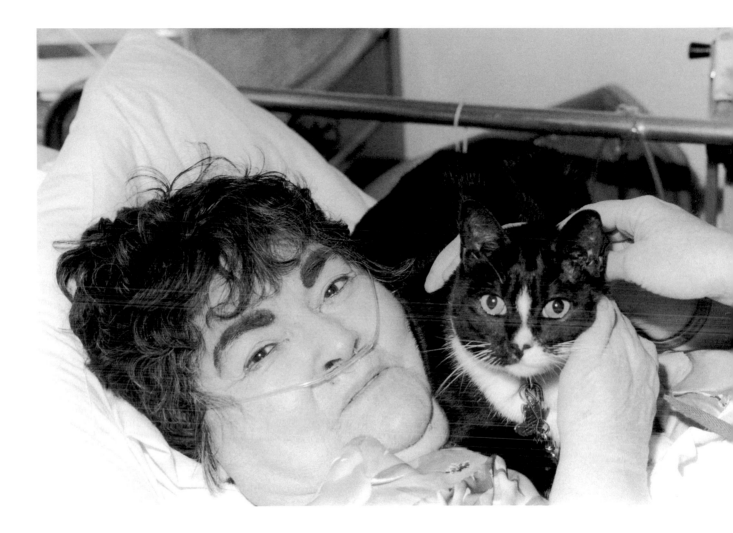

Sonrisa (Sonny), a horse adopted by the Helen Woodward Animal Center, has riders of all ages. Robin Cohen (right) assists riders with their exercises while handling the horses.

In addition to her standard physical therapy, this girl's progress also results from therapeutic riding. "The riding therapy is so good for her, and rubbing the horses is also helpful," says her mother proudly.

PAWS/LA volunteer Meredith Gibbs delivers food and supplies to many pets whose owners have HIV and AIDS throughout Los Angeles County.

PAWS/LA

Los Angeles, California

One Monday morning I met with the staff of PAWS/LA (Pets Are Wonderful Support/Los Angeles) in their West Hollywood office for a different sort of photo shoot. PAWS/LA helps people living with HIV and AIDS keep and care for their pets. Although pets are a great source of support and love, caring and providing for a pet can be next to impossible due to financial and physical constraints for those with the disease. For this reason, PAWS/LA has a dedicated group of volunteers, veterinarians, groomers, and staff helping clients to maintain their pets' health and happiness, giving them the security of knowing they won't lose their pets.

I waited for a few minutes for a volunteer to arrive at the office. As I looked at photos lining the walls of clients and their pets, Nadia Sutton, a cofounder of PAWS/LA, greeted me as she walked by with "Bonjour." My years of French lessons had faded long ago, and I responded with a humble "hello."

Nadia's friend who had AIDS told her that his family had to give his cat away during the time he was in the hospital. He then added that he had no reason to get better and no desire to return home. Nadia found and returned the cat to her friend who was able to spend his last six months with his favorite companion. Incidents like these inspired her and a group of others to begin PAWS/LA in 1989. Often people with AIDS will neglect themselves in order not to lose their pets. They refuse medical treatment to stay home with their pet, divert monies for their pet's needs, or even starve to ensure their pet can eat. Keeping those living with the disease from having to choose between taking care of themselves or taking care of their pet is the mission of PAWS/LA. Pets are the only family members some people have left.

Volunteers walk dogs, change litter boxes and bird cages, take pets to the veterinarian or to grooming appointments, deliver pet food to homebound clients, or provide temporary homes while a client is hospitalized. PAWS/LA funds routine and emergency veterinary care, spaying or neutering, annual vaccinations, grooming services, and pet food, and, for those who qualify, PAWS/LA provides pet security deposits. PAWS/LA also provides educational information on pet care and special precautions for those with HIV and AIDS. Back in the office, the PAWS/LA staff works continuously matching volunteers with clients, scheduling necessary appointments, and processing new requests. PAWS/LA relies on private donations of money and pet food, grants, and fundraising events in order to accommodate their clients. Further support through celebrity volunteers and functions has gained considerable exposure for the organization.

With a love for animals and a compassion for those living with HIV and AIDS, Meredith Gibbs began volunteering with PAWS/LA in 1996. Having had friends with AIDS and owning horses and dogs, her experience benefits those she visits, and adds value to the precious time she donates. Volunteers not only bring pet food and supplies, they bring conversation, opportunities to share stories, and companionship.

Meredith was packing her van with dog food when I approached. When she was done, we both left in the van to visit Joe Monroe and his Italian Greyhound, Jaxson. I helped her with the canned food, and we entered the lobby. Jaxson was there to thank us for the delivery, he knew the nature of our visit, and led the way up the stairs to meet his owner.

Joe is a local artist, and his sunny apartment also serves as his studio. His paintings are large and colorful and, ironically, are inspired by AIDS, which he has lived with since 1984. In between posing for my photographs, Joe buzzed from room to room chasing an energetic Jaxson, gathering material for us to look at, and showing us his paintings. There was a lot of energy in the room. A longtime friend of Nadia's, Joe is forever grateful for the chance to hold onto Jaxson during the darkest moments of his fight with the disease. In return, he feels fortunate to be able to offer his artistic talents for projects such as PAWS/LA greeting cards and Christmas ornaments.

Along with having AIDS, Joe has survived a bout with cancer, severe back pain, and a list of other problems. He has moved five times, and through it all, PAWS/LA was there to help him care for Jaxson. "When I'm in the hospital, they find someone to take care of Jaxson. A vet came out for Jaxson and PAWS/LA paid for it. Every time I need them, they're here. They've allowed me to have him."

For all of the support Jaxson gives, Joe appreciates an opportunity to help his friend, too. "Sometimes Jaxson has seizures, and I'll hold him and talk him out of it...He's like the lover that allows me not to get involved so much that it could take me away from my health regime. Having AIDS is a fulltime job. He allows me to have that emotional connection and lets me take care of my health at the same time."

Jaxson greeted Meredith and me in the lobby of Joe Monroe's apartment. Jaxson seemed to know the nature of our visit, and showed us where to take his food.

Joe shows Meredith (left) illustrations that he contributes to a Los Angeles magazine. Joe and his friend, Jaxson, pose in front of one of Joe's paintings in his studio apartment (right).

Romer, a black Labrador Retriever, a former assistance dog for Canine Companions for Independence (CCI), is now a "facility dog" for CCI. Romer and his owner Barbara Richman help this patient achieve her goals at Scripps Memorial Hospital Encinitas.

Hospital Rounds

Encinitas, California

In the Rehabilitation Center of Scripps Memorial Hospital Encinitas, a patient is working on the range of motion in her arm. Today Romer, a retired assistance dog with Canine Companions for Independence (CCI) and now a 'facility dog' through CCI, will assist with her physical therapy. In addition to standard physical therapy exercises, Nancy Stern, Recreational Therapist at the hospital since 1995, likes the incentive the dogs offer to the animal-assisted therapy (AAT) program, which was introduced to the hospital in 1991. "When we ask patients to work on their exercises, they see it as more of a task, but to incorporate petting a dog into the exercises, it creates more incentive as well as being a natural response. The dogs also stimulate conversation between therapist and patient, and patients tend to forget their anxiety. They become more physically motivated to perform their exercises."

Romer is owned by Barbara Richman, a CCI volunteer, puppy raiser, and facility dog graduate with Romer. She acquired Romer in 1998 after Romer's five year career as an assistance dog ended. Barbara and Romer visit many facilities together and are committed to easing the pain of others. They also serve as a valuable resource for health professionals like Nancy who likes Romer to participate in patient group exercises and individual sessions, and escorts Romer and Barbara from room to room.

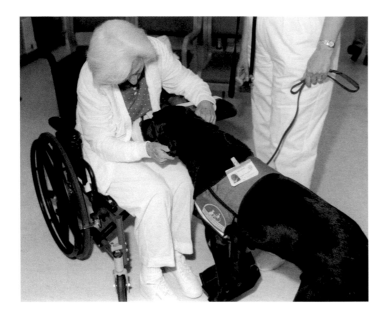 

Romer encourages patients to work on therapeutic exercises. Rubbing a pet can increase range of motion for those with limited movement.

When I volunteer with

Romer, I know I'm making

a difference *in someone's life, and that's important. — Barbara Richman,*

Canine Companions for Independence volunteer

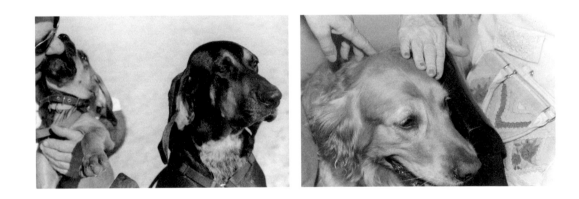

The same comforts and companionship our pets provide us at home or during a walk (left) can benefit those in nursing homes (right) healthcare facilities, and other institutions.

Pets can be therapeutic in any environment.

They are soothing fixtures around the house and yard, and after a difficult day, they can offer diversion, like taking a walk in the park. They invite passers-by to smile. They keep us company. They listen and sometimes seem to understand. When we cannot embrace the people in our lives, we can stop to embrace a pet.

Thankfully, these living sources of comfort are now welcomed regulars in healthcare facilities and other institutions. While visiting the facilities featured in this book, I saw the loneliness that can prevail within these places — places where before I had feared to enter. Winding through corridors and into the rooms of strangers, I witnessed scenes that were at times disturbing and difficult to comprehend, and I saw the difference that animals can make.

That experience has broadened my understanding of the relationships between people and animals at home — wherever home may be.

Thomas provides animal-assisted therapy at home. His owners' comments:
"He puts his head on my knee, I rub his face, and he comforts me," says Jim.
Betsy adds that, "it doesn't matter what mood I'm in when I come home,
he's always happy to see me."

resources

for further information on AAT guidelines, certification, and education

Delta Society
289 Perimeter Road East
Renton, WA 98055
800.869.6898
www.deltasociety.org

Organizations Featured

Green Mountain Humane Society
P.O. Box 1426
White River Junction, VT 05001
802.296.7297

Therapy Dogs Incorporated
P.O. Box 5868
Cheyenne, WY 82003
877.843.7364
www.therapydogs.com

Helen Woodward Animal Center
6461 El Apajo Road
P.O. Box 64
Rancho Santa Fe, CA 92067
www.animalcenter.org
858.756.4117

Therapy Dogs International, Inc.
88 Bartley Road
Flanders, NJ 07836
973.252.9800
www.tdi-dog.org

PAWS/LA
7315 Santa Monica Blvd.
West Hollywood, CA 90046-6615
www.pawsla.org
323.876.7297

Canine Companions for Independence
P.O. Box 446
Santa Rosa, CA 95402-0446
800.572.2275
www.caninecompanions.org

Pet-A-Pet Club, Inc.
P.O. Box 40201
Redford, MI 48239
313.535.0410

Canine Good Citizen (CGC)
850.877.2901
cgc@akc.org

131